HARTMUT VON CZAPSKI

AF190306

Qi Gong sitting

Not only for the disabled and handicapped,
also for office workers.

HARTMUT VON CZAPSKI

Qi Gong sitting

Not only for the disabled and handicapped,
also for office workers.

IMPRESSUM

Bibliographic information of the German National Library: The German National Library lists this publication in the German National Bibliography, and detailed bibliographic data are available on the Internet at http://dnb.dnb.de.

© 2019 Hartmut von Czapski

Pictures: Ellen von Czapski und Hartmut von Czapski

Production and publishing: BoD – Books on Demand, Norderstedt
ISBN: 9783750431409

Table of Contents

Foreword

These exercises are suitable for use in the office, in old peoples home or for home use, when Qi Gong exercises are too exhausting when standing up. But even after a one-hour Qi Gong training while standing, these stretching massage and breathing exercises are gladly accepted. The fact that they are performed while sitting does not mean that they are not exhausting.

The increased oxygen uptake and the stretching of the tendons and muscles are initially unfamiliar. That is why, especially with older sick people, sometimes less is more. Each one according to his ability. The skills improve over time.

This is neither a book about Chinese medicine, Chinese philosophy or acupuncture. It is oriented to the practice. Whether one knows or accepts Chinese philosophy is helpful in these exercises, but not essential. The exercises unfold their effect, whether one believes in it or not.

About the author

Hartmut von Czapski

Non-medical practitioner since 1984. Since 1987 exercise of acupuncture (Teacher Fr.Dr. Li Te, Chief Physician Nankei Clinic). Several stays in China with professional trainings.

1987 Scientific training of Uni.Tübingen passed: "Ecology and its biological basis".

Since1990 seminars, yoga and Qi Gong courses at various institutes. Since 1990 more than 1000 Qi Gong classes have been held.

Qi Gong Teacher 49009 des Mi Gong Rulai Buddhist Center for Qi Gong, Shanghai.

Training to Qi Gong Therapeut by Prof. Wu, Shanghai.

Lectures at the Medica in Dusseldorf on the treatment of incontinence with T.C.M .

1999 acupuncture specialist training for dentists; Teacher activity on various therapies.

Teaching Qi Gong Forms:

Medical Qi Gong according to Prof. Wu.

Taiji Qigong after Li Ding.

Ten meditations on the mountain Wudang.

The Eighteenfold Method of Exercise.

The "Movements of the 5 Animals".

Qi Gong after Guo Lin for immune boosting.

The "Eight elegant exercises. "

"Wai dan gung"

Tai Chi for beginners by Dr. med. Jiang Hao-quan. And much more.

Qi Gong

The term "Qi Gong" includes various types of exercises to absorb the "Qi", the life energy, and let it flow in the energy channels, the so-called "meridians". It is a substance that you normally do not see and grope, but can feel. The ancient Chinese philosophers thought that Qi is a source substance that originated in the Big Bang.

According to the Chinese view, Qi is a continuously moving and active substance, the basic substance from which the body originates. Qi receives the human life functions. By definition Qi in Qi Gong is an "essence" substance in the body with a certain energy. Qi can be formed, developed, transformed and moved in the body. Breathing moves the energy in the meridians. But even after a long practice of Qi Gong, one can move and absorb qi with the mind in the body.

These body and breathing exercises have at least a 4000-year-old tradition in China, as can be seen in descriptions of funerary offerings. There are many different types of exercises. On the one hand the soft Qi Gong, which contains many meditative elements based on the imagination and is often performed while sitting or lying down. On the other hand, we know the hard Qi Gong, which also strengthens the muscles and tendons and massages the internal organs. Think e.g. to the achievements of the Shaolin monks in Kung Fu or to the acrobatic skills of the actors of Peking Opera. But Qigong exercises not only strengthen the body, but also calm the mind and regulate the autonomic nervous system.

A special form is the therapeutic qigong, which prescribes certain exercises for certain illnesses. Like any empirical science, qigong is always being developed. For example, in recent decades, e.g. certain new exercises against cancer are famous for their good results (Qi Gong after Guo Lin for improving the immune system). The high blood pressure research institute Shanghai has already published in 1978 works with reports on changes that causes Qigong on the ECG and EEG. Work has also been published that our sympathetic nervous system, which is active through prolonged stress, achieves relaxation through Qi Gong by predominance of the parasympathetic nervous system.

In China, in many hospitals, in addition to the Department of Medicine, there is a Department of Traditional Chinese Medicine. This includes the treatment room for the Qi Gong therapist. Here the patient is not only taught exercises that he should practice regularly at home, the therapist also supplies the patient with energy that he himself has absorbed. Training to become a Qi Gong therapist is usually tedious. After 5 years of practice, you can teach Qi Gong exercises and also treat after 10 years. Mr. von Czapski has been trained by Prof.Wu as a Qi Gong therapist

Energy intake and delivery points

Yongchuan. When we "dig" the toes into the ground, a hollow is formed below the base toe joints.
Point kidney1.

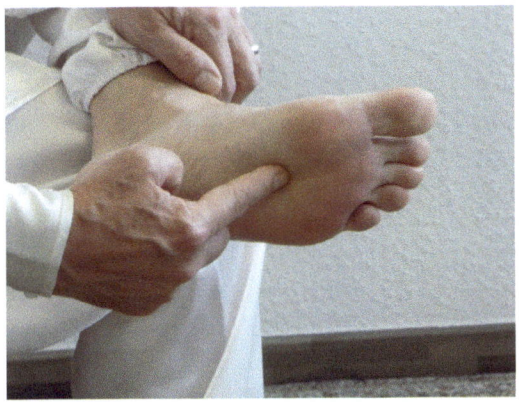

Laogong. If we tilt the fingertip of the ring finger into the palm of the hand, we come to this point.

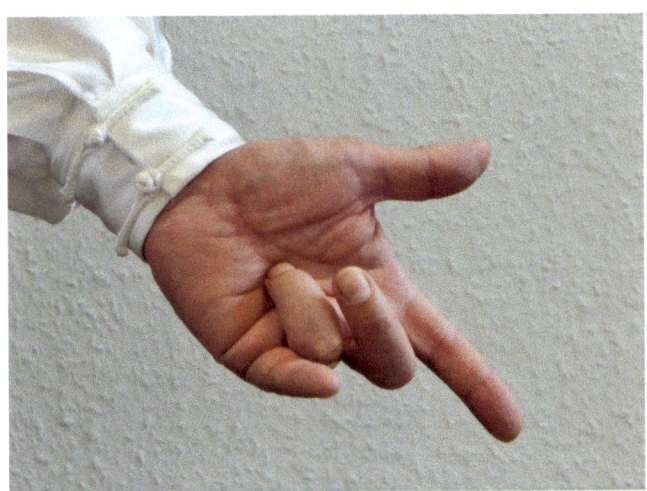

Important energy centers

"Genuine" dantian. Lies between belly button and spine. Lower Dantian, about 2 cross finger wide under the navel. At the height of the acupuncture point "Qi Hai", sea of energy.

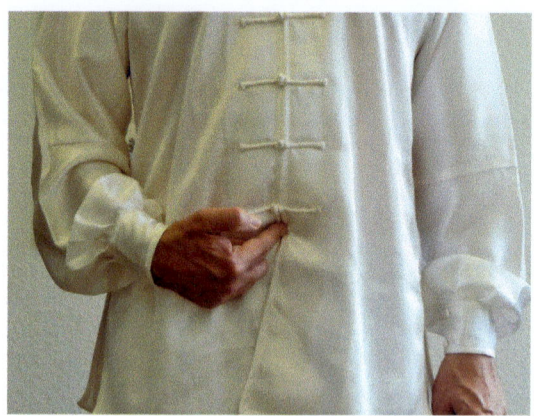

Upper Dantian, Yintang. Between the eyebrows, just above the bridge of the nose.

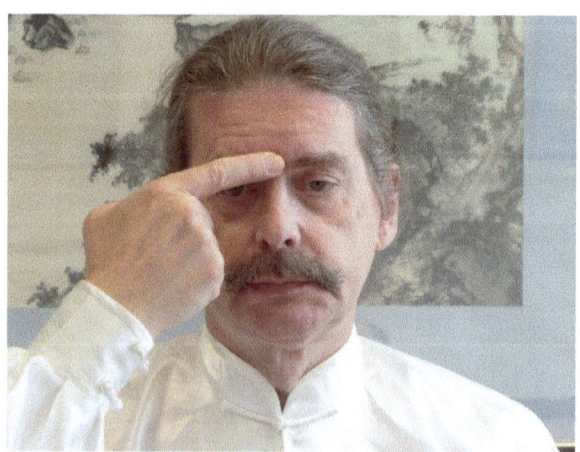

Middle Dantian, Tanzhong, heart center. At the level of a cowl on the sternum, just above the nipples.

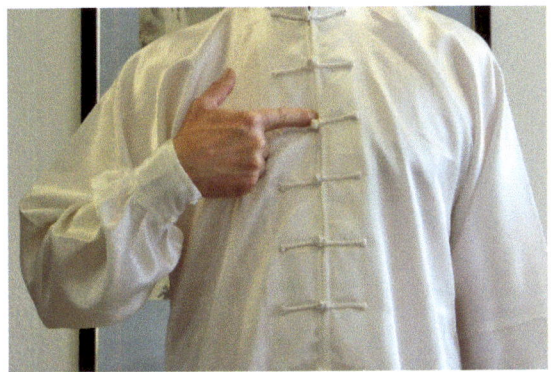

Mingmen. If you put the index finger upper edges under the back ribs and your thumbs stretched towards the spine, you reach with the tips of the thumb to the Mingmen point on the spine.

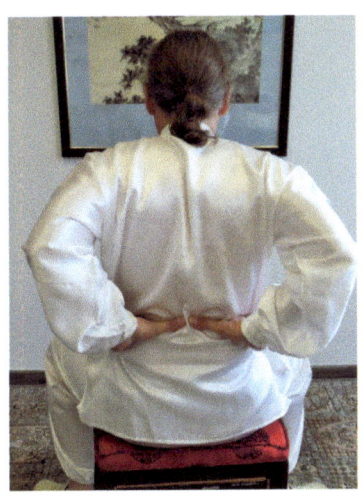

While sitting:
Usually: put hands on thighs. Thighs and lower legs at right angles. Just sitting straight but relaxed. The breathing method is given in the individual exercises.

1) Neck- Crane- Exercise

Normal breathing. Stretch the chin forward, then fold to the chest and pull the chin upwards. The cervical spine is stretched.8x

2) Turn the head in 4 directions

Normal breathing. Looking straight ahead, then tilt the chin to the chest and look there too.

Then backwards, look up and then back to the starting position.

Next turn your head slowly to the left and look backwards on our personal horizon. That means do not look up or down. Pay attention to the personal limit. Do not force anything by force, no jerky movements. Then turn your head forward again. Turn right, look to the right horizon, then back to the middle.

Repeat 3 times.

3) Massage the head

Normal breathing. Massage the scalp with the fingertips of both hands from front to back. This is in the course of the head meridians. 8x.

4) Knock the head

Normal breathing. With loose fingers of both hands, knock the head, the neck and the shoulders, from front to back. 8x. Then rub the transition from cervical to thoracic spine. With the right hand and then with the left hand.

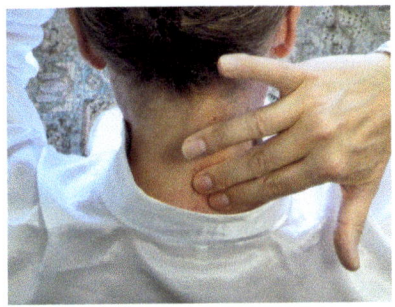

5) Skydrums

Normal breathing. Place the middle fingers on the back end of the skull so that the palms are above the ears. Place the index fingers on the middle fingers and then flick them into the underlying coolers. There is the point G20 which is used in many head complaints, e.g. Vision and hearing problems, headaches and so on.

The skull acts like a drum and ideally a drum noise is heard.

Another type of sky drum: Use the middle finger to press the tragus onto the ear canal. Drum on the middle finger with the index finger. The sound waves stimulate acupuncture points around the ear that are effective against diseases of the ears.

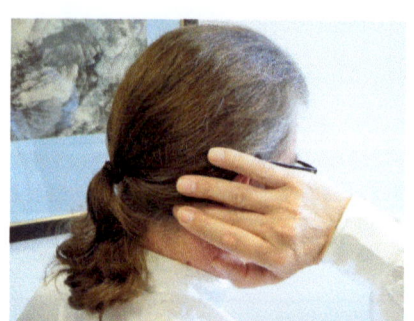
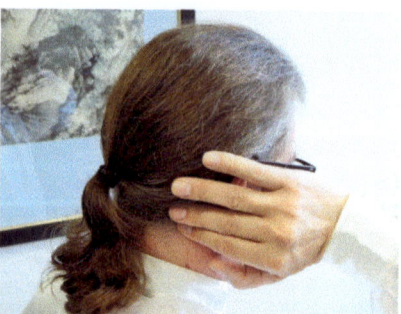

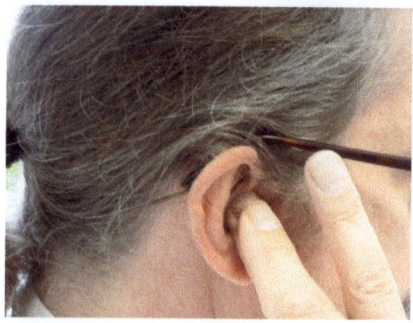

6) Shoulder massage

Normal breathing. When we pull our shoulders forward, we get a cowl under the collarbone. There is the second point of the lung meridian. We push our index and middle fingers into this cave and then move our fingers straight up over our shoulders to the back. We run from back to front across the upper arm and over a hollow under the muscle belly (about half of the distance shoulder- elbow).
Repeat 16 times, then the other side. This exercise is not only good for the shoulder, it also stimulates breathing and defenses by stimulating the lung meridian.

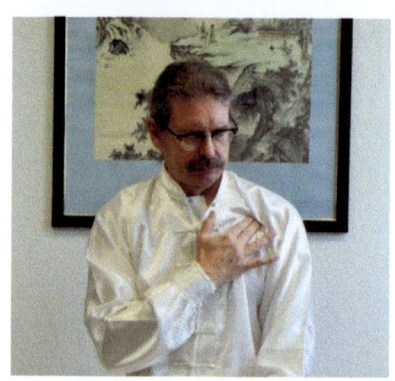

7) Meridian massage

Normal breathing. Begin with the palms on your hips. Lower your hands sideways, down to your knees or up to the outer ankle, depending on your ability. Change to the inside of the legs. Brush up on the inside of the legs. Over the midline of the body up to the neck. Swipe around the neck, from the front to the back of the neck, then over the back of the head, forehead and face. Over the breastbone to the ribs to the right and left. Continue back to the kidneys. From there to the beginning, to the hips. 8x.

8) Archery

With both hands, spread the index finger and the thumb, fold in the other fingers. Put the right wrist over the left breast.

Extend right arm to the right, inhale. The index finger points upwards (the wood). Extend the left elbow to the left until shoulder level. The index finger points to the right (the tendon). The bow is stretched. Target an imaginary target with your right index finger, "shoot" and exhale, placing your right hand on the chest first, the left one above. Wrist over wrist.

Extend left arm to left, inhale, s.o. 8x to the right and 8x to the left.

9) Knee massage

Normal breathing. With forefinger and middle finger 16 times, in each direction to massage the kneecaps circular. Then rub your index and middle fingers up and down in the back of your knees. Good for the knees, lumbar spine and strength of the legs.

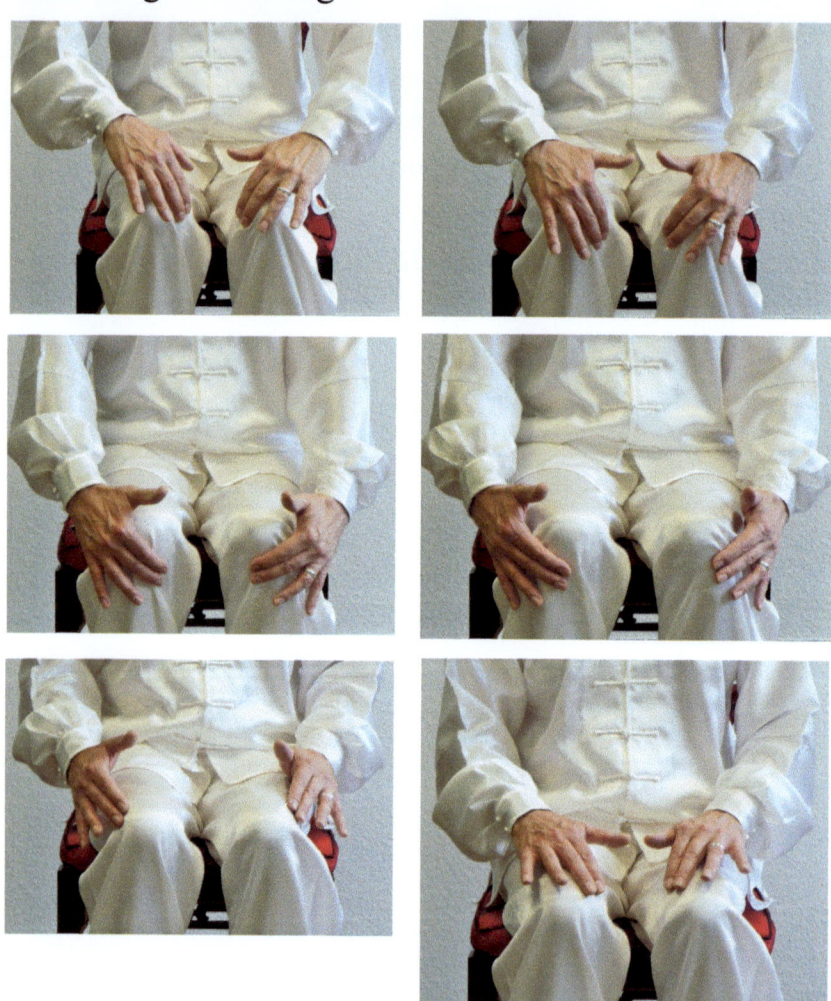

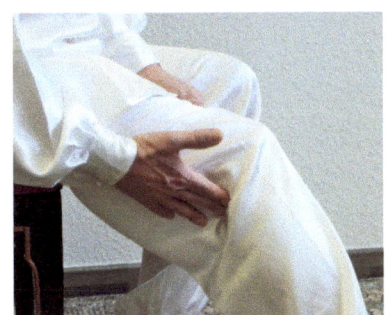 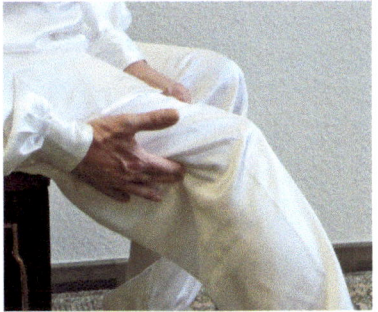

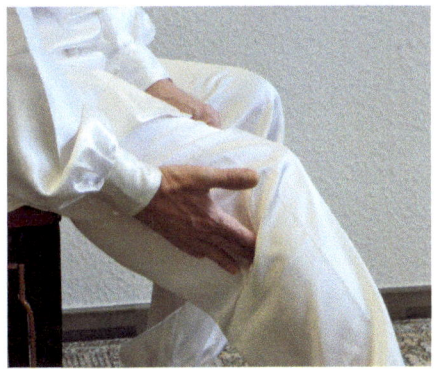

10) Rub kidneys

Normal breathing. Use both hands in the kidney area (lower ribs, costal arch) to rub it up and down until it warms up.

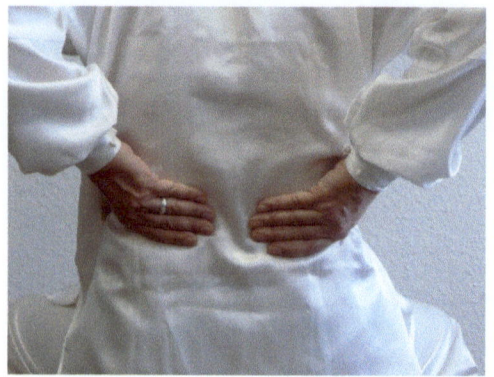

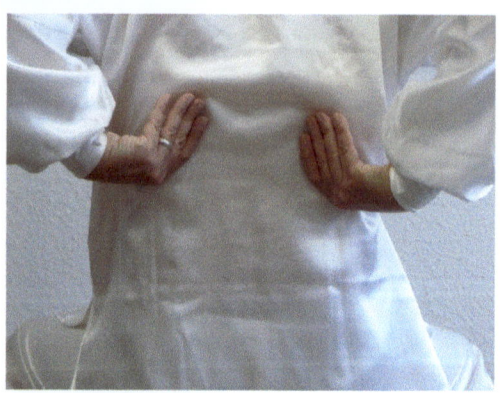

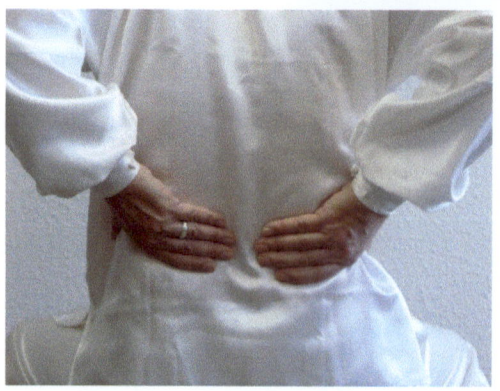

11) Elbow to the knee

Clasped hands behind head, elbows forward. Inhale, then simultaneously raise one knee and bring the elbow of the other side of the body and the knee together. Exhale. When going back, inhale again.

12) Rub Yongchuan

Normal breathing. Rub the point kidney1 (yongchuan) with your index and middle fingers. The movement goes from the cowl under the toe joints aslant down towards the inner ankle. Hold your left foot with your left hand and massage with the fingers of your right hand. 100 times quickly. Then vice versa. Soothes the nervous system and promotes drainage. There are warm feet in winter. aslant

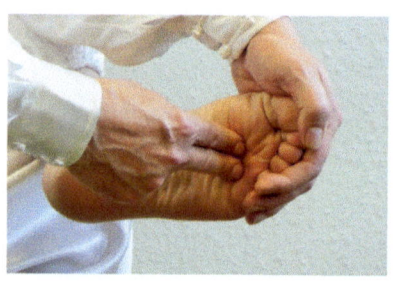
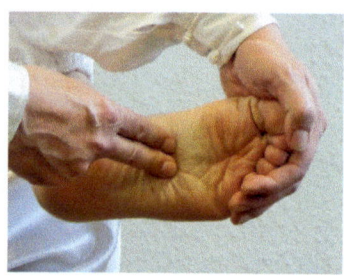

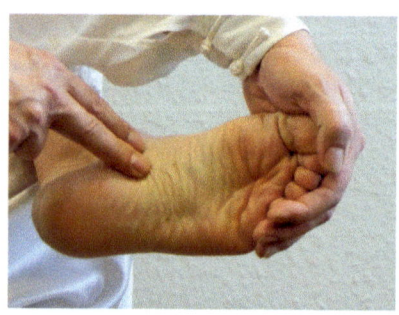
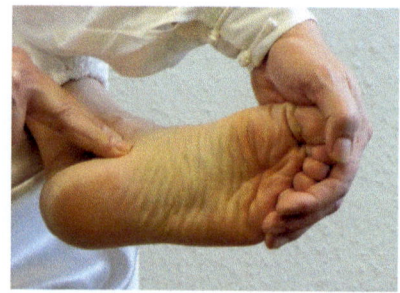

13) Feet circling, toes pulling up

Both feet, from the ankle, rotate 8x clockwise. Then 8 circles counterclockwise.
Pull the toes of both feet 8x upwards towards the body.
Inhale. Let go and exhale.

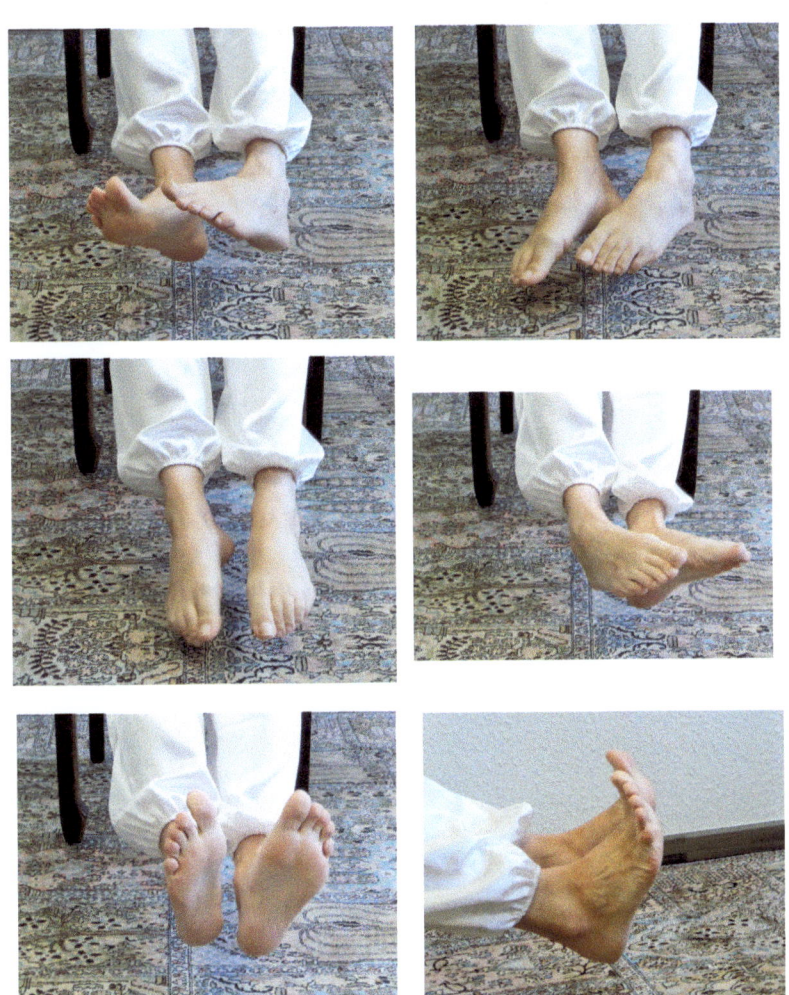

14) Turn the winch

Keep loose fists next to your shoulders. Describe large circles with your fists, upwards and downwards. Exhale. Breathe in straighten and raising fists. 8x.

Then raise one hand up and look there and stretch the other fist down. As we lower one hand with an extended arm, we lift the other hand with an extended arm. We always look up to the lifted hand. A movement like scratching in the water.

We breathe in on one side, exhale on the other side. Depending on your ability, we can lean forward or sit straight. Look 4x to each side.

15) Let shoulders rotate

Both shoulders rotate in opposite directions.
8x clockwise, 8x against.

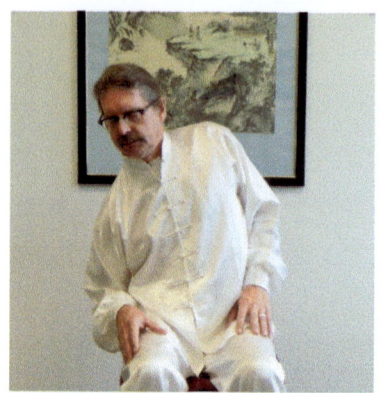 

16) To offer qi

Both hands, close together, stretch forward. Palms upwards. Exhale.

Turn palms outwards and move hands outstretched, inhaling. Then bring your hands tightly under your armpits, palms up, stretch forward and exhale. 8x.

 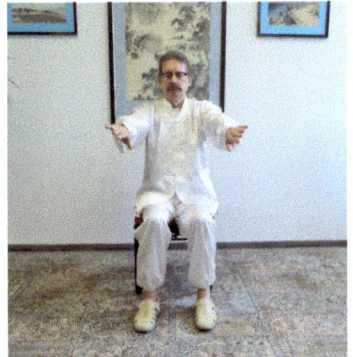

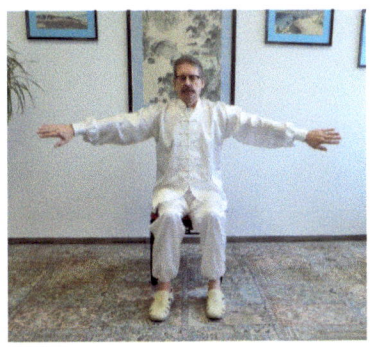 

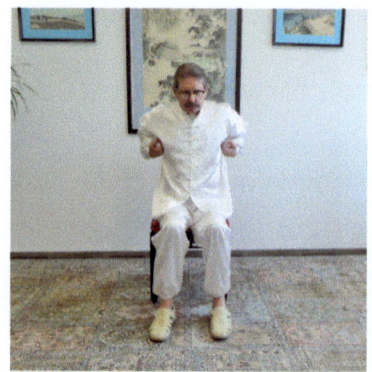 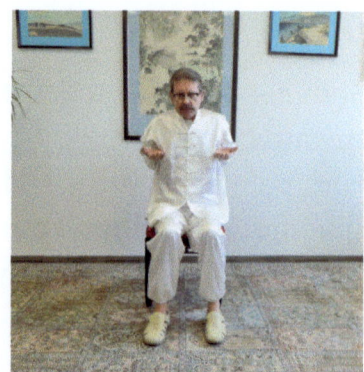

17) Circling the upper body

Move forward on the seat. Move with the upper body to the left and front, while exhaling. Continue the circle to the right and up, breathing in. 8 circles clockwise, 8 circles counterclockwise. When circling after obtuse upper body also lead something backwards, which strengthens the abdominal muscles. Important: Fix a point on the floor during the whole exercise, otherwise you will become dizzy.

The digestive organs are massaged, strengthened back and abdominal muscles.

18) Put on the knees

Put one knee as close to the torso as possible, inhale and spread out the arms, palms upwards.

Lower leg, put hands on thighs and exhale. 4 times every side.

Affects the respiratory and digestive organs.

19)Paint circle

We imagine a pane of glass in front of us. We use the palms of our hands to draw a large circle on this glass. When leading up the hands we do not extend the arms completely, so that the arms also form a circle in the elevated state. The gaze moves in the middle with the upward and downward movement up and down. As we move upwards, we breathe deeply into the chest, moving the energy upwards. During the declining movement we exhale, the energy sinks downwards. Improves lung capacity and oxygen uptake.8x.

20) Face massage

Normal breathing. Both thumbs with the fists enclose. Rub the thumb backs until they get hot. Then rub the sides of the nose up and down with the backs of the thumbs. Then press the fingertips of the index finger next to the nostrils. Count to 30, then solve; Repeat 3 times. Find the transition from the bony nostril to the upper jaw, press with the fingernails of the index finger into this gap. Count to 30, then redeem. 3x. This massage is good for all sinuses.

Rub the thumb backs and rub the knuckles over the eyes. Extend over the eyelids from the inner corner of the eye.16x.

Rub the thumb backs and stroke over the eyebrows. From the nose to the outside. 16x.

For headaches, eye diseases, sinuses, colds.

Massage the face with the fingertips of the index and middle fingers. Start over the eyes, around the eyes until just under the eyes. Then pull down, around the corners of the mouth around to the chin.
8x in this direction, then massage 8x from bottom to top. For wrinkling, headache, good for the teeth, eyes, facial muscles.

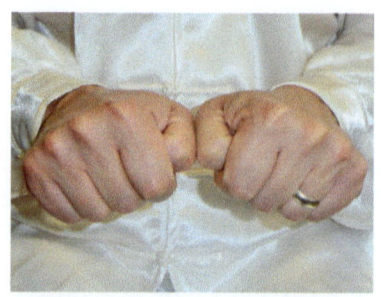 

 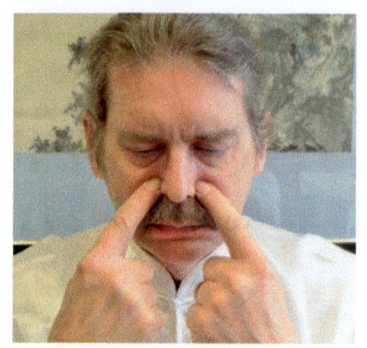

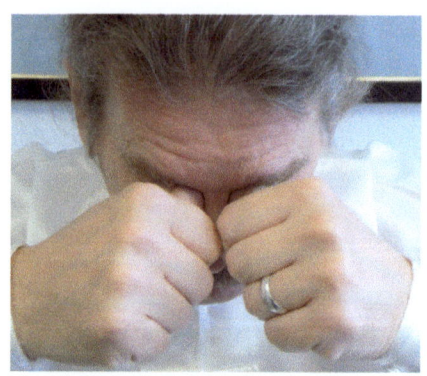 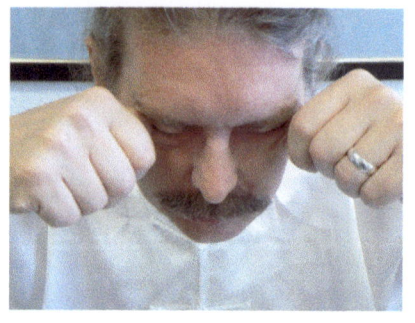

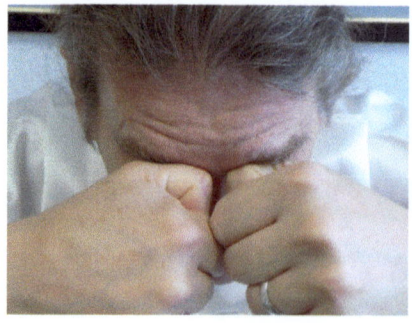 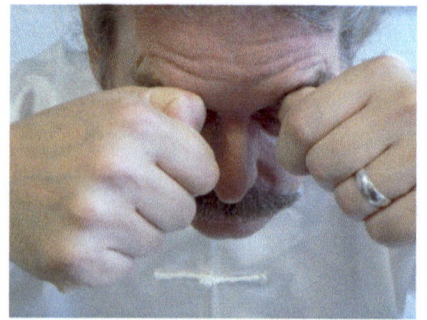

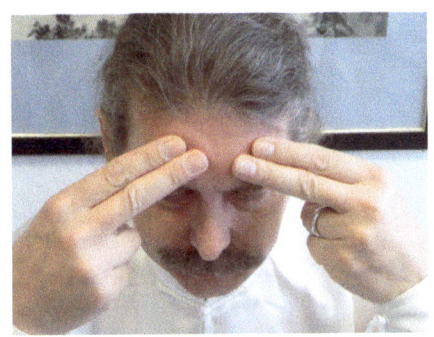 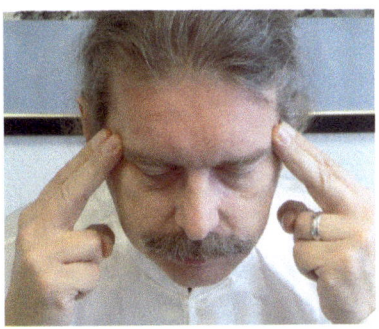

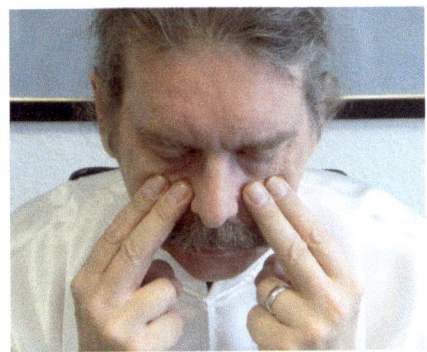 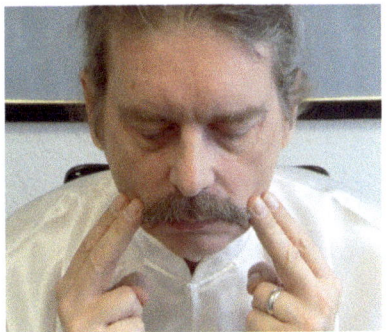

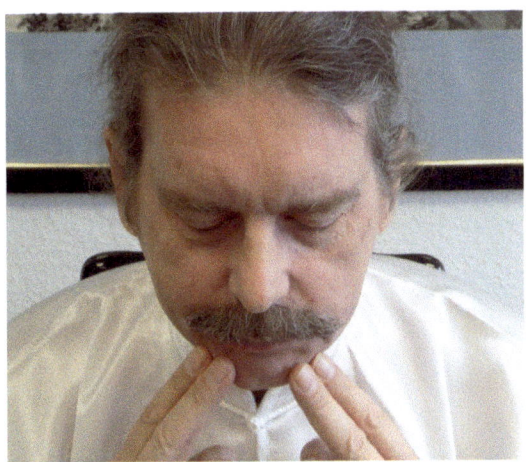

21) Eyes circle

Normal breathing. Turn your eyes clockwise 8x without moving the head. Then circle 8 times counterclockwise.
Close your eyes tight, then tear wide. Good for the circulation of the eyes and eye muscles.

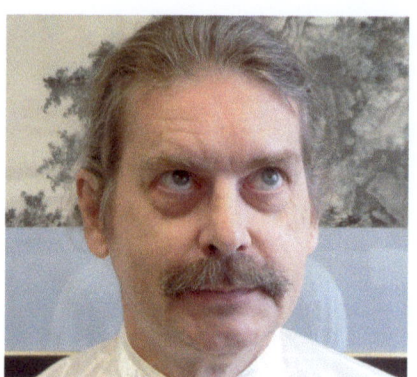 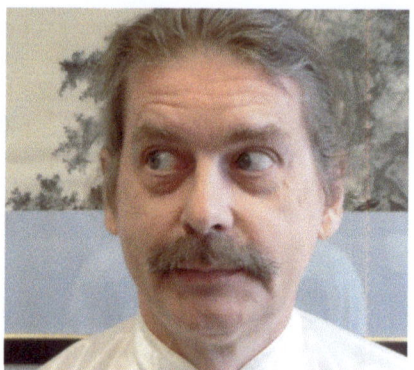

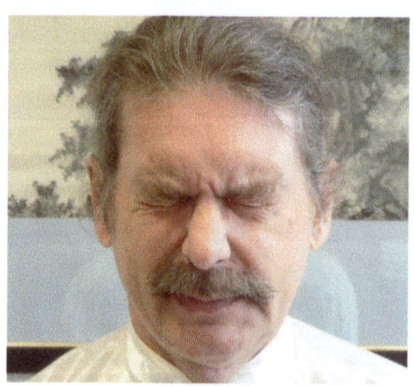 

22) Massage ears

Normal breathing. With the index finger and the thumb, grasp the upper ear edge and massage the ear edge from top to bottom to the earlobe with gentle circular movements.

Then with the index finger in the pinna from top to bottom. Repeat both 16 times.

With index finger and middle finger behind the ear and with ring finger and little finger in front of the ear rup up and down. 16X

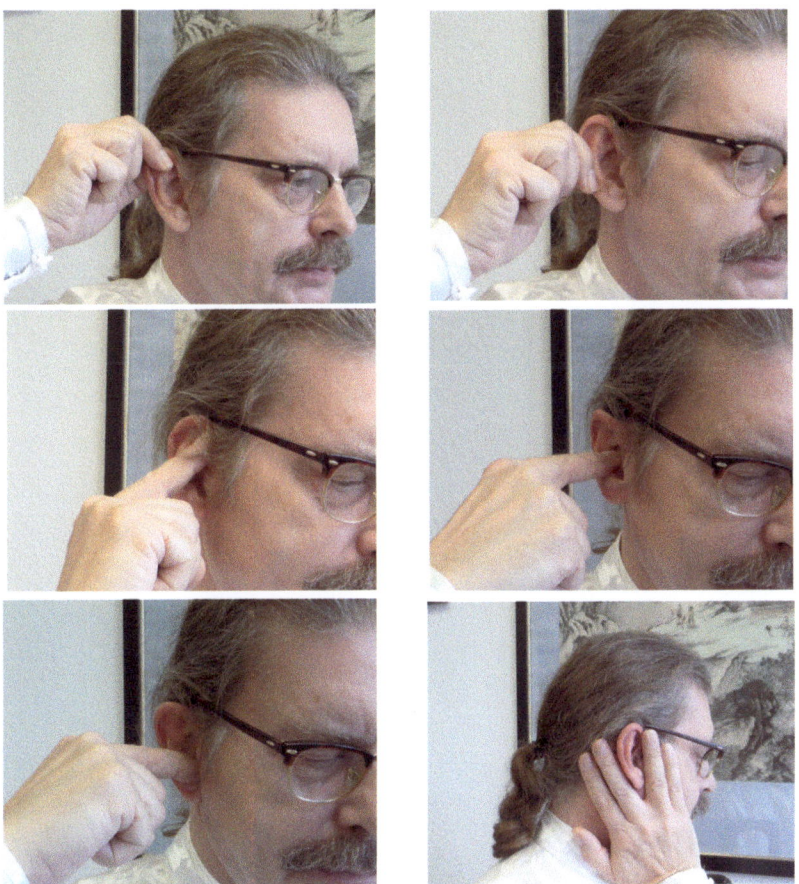

23) Lead the qi up and down

Place both hands cupped under the belly button. Inhale and raise both hands to the level of the heart. Turn over hands, exhale and press hands down to the lower abdomen. 8x

24) Stretch the fist to the sky

Keep both fists in front of each other, exhale. Stretch
your left fist diagonally to the sky, stretch your right
elbow diagonally to the lower right, look to the lower
right, inhale. Exhale again when merging the fists. 8x.
Then stretch your right fist diagonally upwards and so
on.

25) Yin and Yang

Hold the right hand over the head, hold the left behind the back. Exhale. As you inhale, move your right hand down to the left, we are looking down to the left, the left hand is moving to the right rear. Change hands with the exhale. The left hand over the head, the right behind the back. As you inhale, move your left hand down to the right, we are looking down to the right, the right hand is moving to the left behind.

26) Pull elbows apart and rotate

Keep both fists together in front of chest, exhale. Keep elbows aside, breathing in and expanding your chest. Exhale again when merging the fists. 8x.
Both fists in front of the chest against each other. Stretch one elbow diagonally downwards and extend the other elbows diagonally upwards. Then use this elbow to describe 8 circles in a clockwise direction and 8 circles in a counterclockwise direction. Breathing normal.

27) Support the sky

Lead the arms up and to the right in the arch and inhale. Fingers cross, stretch upwards "Support the sky" and exhale. Looking forward again. When inhaling, the hands go back the same way.

28) Abdominal massage

Women put their right hands under their navels, men put their left hands. We put the other hand over it so that we cover the wrist from above. Hands pressed against stomach, stomach against hands. We are doing 8, increasing circles in a clockwise direction. Up to the ribs, the belly sides, the pubis and so on. We stop over the pubis and then make 8 smaller and smaller circles counterclockwise. With each upward movement we breathe in, with every downward movement we breathe out.1-2 times. After each exercise put both hands on the lower abdomen and feel.

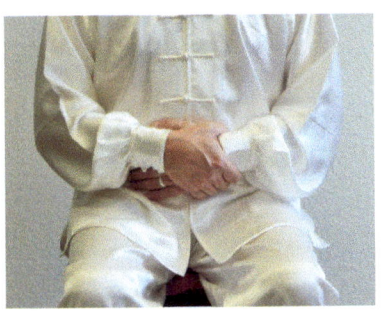 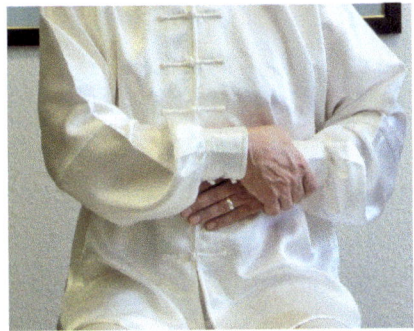

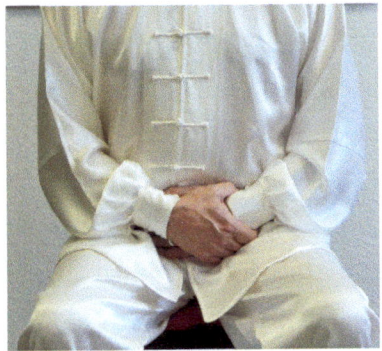 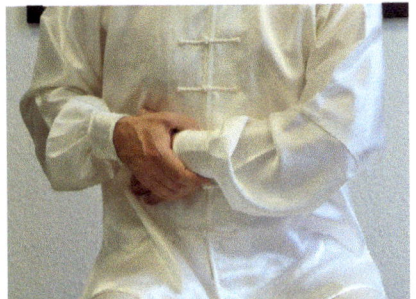

29) Boxing

Form 1

The thumbs with the fists enclose, with the inside of the fist upwards on the pelvic bones.

When breathing in, push your right fist forward, half way down turn your inner fist down and exhale.

Inhale and bring back the right fist, turning it again while pushing the left fist forward, while breathing out, put the right fist on the hip while turning the left fist (fist inside down) and push forward. So continue in a constant change.

Form 2

The thumbs with the fists enclose, with the inside of the fist upwarts on the pelvic bones.
When breathing in, push your right fist forward; up to half of the possible stretching movement.
While exhaling, turn the inside of the fist forward and push, opening your hand.
When inhaling, reverse the previous movement; up to half of the possible stretching movement.
While exhaling, put your fist back on the pelvic bones.When inhaling, extend your left fist, see above.
When pushing the fist forward, the upper arm and upper body should form a right angle. Do not turn your shoulders forward and your back should stay straight. It depends on the inner strength, not on the outer. Focus on Laogong. 8x each side.

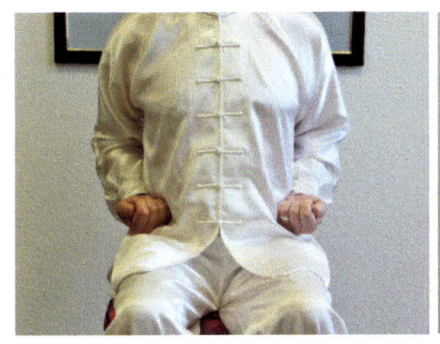 

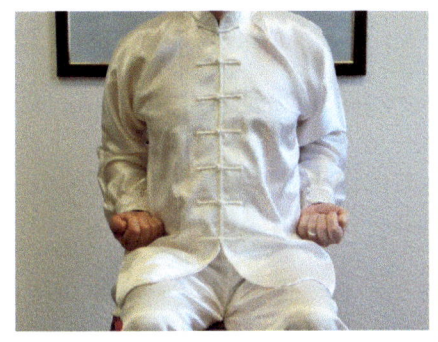

30) 3 routes relaxation (Fang Song Gong)

Concentrate on the mentioned body parts and think "relax" with the exhale.

1) sides of the head, sides of the neck, shoulders, upper arms, elbows, forearms, hands and fingers.
1-2min. focus on the middle finger.

2) Face, neck, chest, abdomen, front of thighs, knees, front of lower legs, front of feet and toes. 1-2 min. focus on the big toes.

3) Back of the head, cervical spine, upper back, middle back, lower back, buttocks and back of the thighs, backside of the knees, calves, heels, soles. Then 1-2min. focus on Yongchuan.

4) Short Run: Concentrating on larger body areas. Head, arms, chest, stomach, legs

5) Focus on a personal problem area or local tension. Relax with the exhale. Repeat several times.

6) Shower: To imagine with the exhalation that an "energy shower" flows from the top down over the body like water.

31) Build up energy field between your hands

Every body has an energy field around it. Whether you call it biophoton radiation or aura. We want to reinforce this energy field with the following exercise.

Both palms against each other hold without touching. We concentrate on the space between the hands. With the inhalation, pull your hands apart, almost bringing your hands together again with the exhale. Imagine you have a soft, half-filled balloon between your hands that you pull apart or squeeze together.Then hold your hands with a little distance above a sick part of your body or above Dantian and Tanzhong. Focus on the distance.

32) Regulated breathing

Just sit down, let your shoulders loose. Just breathe through the nose.

In this exercise you think the sentence: "I am sitting calmly relaxed"

"I am.." inhaling.

"..sitting .." holding the air.

"..calmly relaxed." exhaling.

If you want to do it especially well, you should place the tip of the tongue behind the upper row of teeth while inhaling and holding the air. Release with exhalation. The special meridians "the Great and the Little Governor" are thus united. They run on the midline across the back and front of the Body.

33) Abdominal breathing

In the case of abdominal breathing, the stomach is stretched slightly forward during inhalation, and it is easily drawn in on exhalation. One breathes only with the abdomen, not with the chest. Relaxes and intensifies Qi in Dantian. Harmonious, do not breathe too hard. 20 x inhale and exhale. Soothes the autonomic nervous system, promoting sleep. Beginners should practice sitting or lying down. The first time it helps to put one hand on the stomach and the other on the chest.

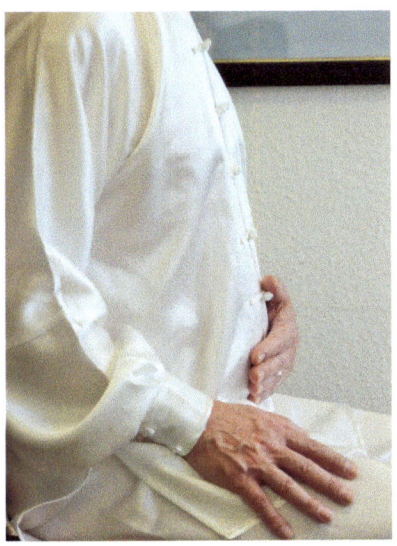 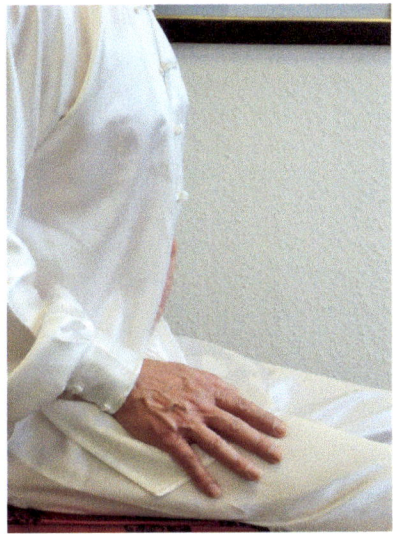

34) Flowers in the hands

Place your hands like 2 open bowls in the groins; on the inside of the thighs. Imagine flowers in the hands. No matter if one or many, real existing or fantasy flowers. When the thoughts drift away, return again and again to the sentence: "Flowers in the hands". Promotes concentration and renal meridian. From the condition and the color of the flowers, something can be learned about the emotional state of the person.

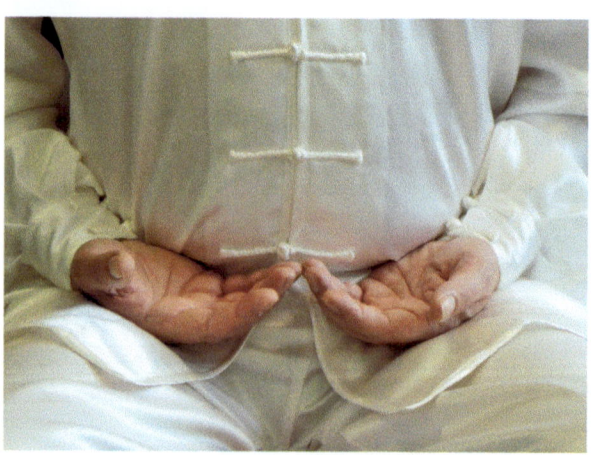

The following Qi Gong books by Hartmut von Czapski will soon be published by the same publisher.

Taiji Qi Gong

This book describes 22 Taiji Qi Gong exercises. These exercises improve the energy intake, strengthen the self-healing powers and balance the autonomic nervous system. They promote the ability to concentrate and inner peace. They have a positive effect on the digestive organs, the muscles, the tendons, joints and the spine. The increased oxygen intake strengthens the heart and lungs.

Qi Gong stand exercises

This book describes 23 qigong stand exercises. These exercises improve the energy intake, strengthen the self-healing powers and balance the autonomic nervous system. They promote the ability to concentrate and inner peace. They strengthen the muscles and the tendons. The stand positions of the 5 animals (monkey, deer, bear, tiger, crane) are also suitable for children.

Medical Qi Gong after Prof. Wu

In this book exercises are shown which, among other things in the following symptoms show excellent effects: high and low blood pressure, stomach and intestinal complaints, lung problems, insomnia, nervousness, lack of concentration, lack of energy, back pain and excessive stress.

With regular and persevering practice of Qi Gong, the practitioner can improve his health and find inner peace and relaxation. Since the exercises can be performed with varying degrees of force, they are also suitable for older, weakened people.